Withdrawn

D0936541

MARTHA GRAHAM

Kristin Kessel

rosen central™

The Rosen Publishing Group, Inc., New York

To Kathi-Jo Hubner

Published in 2006 by The Rosen Publishing Group, Inc.
29 East 21st Street, New York, NY 10010

Copyright © 2006 by The Rosen Publishing Group, Inc.

First Edition

Library of Congress Cataloging-in-Publication Data

Kessel, Kristin.
Martha Graham / Kristin Kessel.— 1st ed.
    p. cm. — (The Library of American choreographers)
Includes bibliographical references and index.
ISBN 1-4042-0450-4 (lib. bdg.)
ISBN 1-4042-0644-2 (pbk. bdg.)
1. Graham, Martha—Juvenile literature. 2. Dancers—United States—
Biography—Juvenile literature. 3. Choreographers—United
States—Biography—Juvenile literature.
I. Title. II. Series.
GV1785.G7K47 2006
792.8'2'092—dc22
                                                            2004029318
Manufactured in the United States of America

On the cover: Inset: Martha Graham in 1947. Background: Martha Graham performing *Appalachian Spring* in September 1944.

Contents

Introduction

Dancer. Choreographer. Pioneer. Goddess. These are some of the words that have been used to describe dance legend Martha Graham. The moment she viewed her first dance performance at the age of sixteen, Martha knew that she was meant to dance. Her career lasted more than seventy years, and the influence of her work on the dance world is still felt today. Similar to masters of twentieth-century art and music, Martha Graham's impact on modern American dance is unparalleled.

Martha Graham was one of the pioneers of a new form of dance called modern dance. In the early part of the twentieth century, choreographers rebelling against the stylistic conventions of classical ballet created the first modern dances. These choreographers wanted dance to be recognized as an art form separate and equal to music and theater. They wanted to create dances that were capable of

This image shows Martha Graham performing one of her most famous dance pieces, *Letter to the World*. It is based on the life and work of the American poet Emily Dickinson. Like many of Graham's dances, this piece used her revolutionary movement technique, innovative sculptural theater design, spoken text, and a musical score to explore the emotional life of a famous female character.

expressing the kinds of feelings, thoughts, and images they were experiencing in the new century. They spent much time exploring movement itself as the essence of dance. They evolved many theories about how and why people move.

Many people contributed to this revolution in dance, but Graham's

This dramatic portrait of Martha Graham was taken before the 1940s. Graham would become known as one of the pioneers of American modern dance. Many of the movements in Graham's dances were extremely jagged and expressionistic as opposed to the lyrical movements of the ballet dancers of her era.

contribution is so important that she is often called the mother of American modern dance. Graham wanted to create a uniquely American dance style that would, as she said, "chart a graph of the heart." She developed a unique dance technique and used it to create more than 180 dances that explored a wide range of human emotions. The dances she created were inspired by Greek myths; Native American folklore; the Bible; and American experiences, such as the westward expansion. Her choreography is still performed by dance companies today, including the company that she began and named for herself, the Martha Graham Dance Company.

During a time when women were expected to marry and raise children, Martha Graham became a dancer and choreographer. Though she faced many challenges, including financial hardship, alcohol addiction, and a heartbreaking romantic relationship, Graham stayed strong, stuck to her beliefs, and continued to dance and choreograph. Graham believed that dance was a holy act. It wasn't a question of her desire to dance; she had to dance. Graham's strong will, artistic vision, and dynamic dancing are what propelled her to become a legend.

1 First Lessons

Martha Graham was born on May 11, 1894, in her parents' home in Allegheny, Pennsylvania. She was the eldest of three sisters. Martha's sister Mary was born in 1896, and Georgia (or Geordie) in 1900. Martha also had a brother, William Henry Graham, but he died when he was just eighteen months old.

Martha's father, Dr. George G. Graham, was a doctor with a special interest in mental, emotional, and nervous disorders. Today he would be called a psychiatrist. On April 23, 1893, Dr. Graham married Jane "Jenny" Beers, who was fifteen years younger than he was. Jenny was a direct descendant of the Pilgrims who had arrived in America on the *Mayflower* on November 11, 1620.

Martha loved both her parents very much. Her mother was small and beautiful with long, dark, curly hair. She loved being

An old family portrait shows Martha, one of her sisters, and her mother. Along with her choreography, Graham is well known for some of her famous sayings, such as "Dance is the hidden language of the soul."

a wife and mother. She indulged Martha and her sisters and made them costumes and gave them jewelry to play with in their games of dress-up.

Her father was a handsome man with golden blond hair. He filled their home with carpets and porcelain from the Far East. Later, Martha would be very inspired by Asian art and philosophy. The Greek myths and legends he told Martha and her sisters also inspired many of Martha's ballets. Martha loved to spend time with her father in his office, reading the books in his library, or observing his patients as they sat in the waiting room.

Once, Dr. Graham invited a seventeen-year-old patient to join his family for dinner. Martha noticed the girl's strange body language and her nervousness. After the girl left, Martha asked her father why she behaved so strangely. As Martha stated in her autobiography, *Blood Memory*, Dr. Graham replied, "She was not well and her body was telling us so." Later, as Martha continued to question her father about the visitor, he told her, "Movement never lies." Years later, Martha would remember what her father said when she was striving to create truthful and honest choreography.

Martha described herself as being very stubborn, determined, and strong-willed, traits that she inherited from her father. Dr. and Mrs. Graham had a warm, playful relationship, and Dr. Graham was very attentive to his wife. Dr. Graham's relationship with Martha was a bit different. He treated Martha more like an equal, and the confidence and security this gave Martha would help her in her career.

A World of Theater

Lizzie Prendergast, an Irish girl who had once been a patient of Dr. Graham's, was the children's nanny for many years. She brightened the household with her warm and fun-loving presence. Lizzie loved the theater and would sing songs to the girls from musicals and assist them in their games of dress-up. With Lizzie's musical influence, the girls put on performances and sent invitations to their family. Once Lizzie took Martha and her sisters to a Catholic church, even though the Grahams were Presbyterian. Martha loved the lush robes of the priests and the formal, mysterious ritual she saw there. She viewed the ceremony as being very theatrical. These experiences helped set the scene for Martha's future on stage. However, it wasn't until after seeing her first live performance that Martha would find a world that she had to be part of.

New Home, New Experiences

In 1908, when Martha was fourteen, her brother, William Henry, died unexpectedly, and Martha's sister Mary developed asthma. The Grahams thought that moving to California, where the air was cleaner than in soot-ridden Allegheny, might help Mary. Perhaps they also felt that the bright sunshine in California would ease some of their grief. The Grahams, Lizzie, and Martha's maternal grandmother packed up their belongings and boarded the only train from Pittsburgh to California. The trip took nine days. Although Martha was ill for much of the time, she would later vividly recall the experience of moving out west in her ballet *Frontier*.

Martha was excited to explore her new home in Santa Barbara, California, and experience everything it had to offer. The sea breeze from the Pacific Ocean was so fresh. Martha wanted to drink everything in: the sunlight, the trees, the flowers, and the dolphins that played in the ocean below the bluff outside their home. Martha met many people of Spanish and Asian descent there, too. Both the natural surroundings and the cultural diversity of Santa Barbara fascinated her.

Martha went to Santa Barbara High School, where she did well in her academic courses and in many extracurricular activities, such as basketball, acting, and sewing class. In fact, she became such a good seamstress that she made her own clothes. She also had some of her short stories and plays published in the school's literary magazine. Because of her writing talent, many of Martha's teachers assumed she would become a writer.

An Inspiring Goddess

One day in 1911, Martha noticed a poster advertising

One of Martha Graham's early role models, Ruth St. Denis, is photographed here in 1946. Of this skillful piece, titled *Nautch Dance*, it was said that Miss St. Denis performed it gracefully and with a sense of ease. The spin shown here was so fast, it was necessary for this photo to be taken with a special camera.

a dance performance by Miss Ruth St. Denis, a well-known dancer of the time. Martha showed her parents the stunning picture of Miss St. Denis in her costume for *Radha*, her dance based on a Hindu goddess. The dance concert was to take place in Los Angeles. At that time, there were no commercial airplanes, and it would be a long trip just to go to the theater. But Martha was determined to go. She begged her parents to take her.

Ultimately, Martha's father took Martha by boat to Los Angeles to see the performance. That day, once the curtains at the Mason Opera House opened, Martha's life was forever changed. She

Russian ballet dancer Natalia Makarova performed the dance *Incense* as a special guest artist with the Martha Graham Dance Company in its 1993 New York season. The season paid tribute to Graham's mentor Ruth St. Denis. The magical and atmospheric dance, choreographed and originally performed by St. Denis, featured splendid costumes and wonderful effects such as smoke.

watched Ruth St. Denis perform her famous dances *Cobra*, *Radha*, and *Egypta*.

Martha felt as if she were watching a true goddess. From that moment on, Martha knew that she had to become a dancer.

2 Denishawn and Beyond

Martha Graham graduated from Santa Barbara High School in 1913. At that time, although some women did attend college, many married soon after graduating and began raising families. Most didn't attend college at all and married directly after completing high school. Her parents expected her to continue on to college. However, Graham had a different plan for herself. She surprised her parents by telling them she didn't want to go to a traditional college. Instead, she intended to go to a liberal arts college in Los Angeles, the Cumnock School of Expression.

The Cumnock School of Expression was an experimental college that offered classes in drama, literature, and art. Not long after Graham began her studies there in 1913, her father died unexpectedly. His death was a great tragedy for the family. Suddenly, they had little income, and it was necessary for them to move to a smaller house. Nonetheless,

Graham was able to finish her studies at Cumnock, from which she graduated in 1916. She was twenty-two years old and faced a difficult reality. Usually professional dancers begin their training by the time they are ten years old. Graham was, by most standards, too old to begin dancing. However, she refused to accept any limitations. When Graham learned that her idol, Ruth St. Denis, together with her husband, Ted Shawn, had opened the Denishawn School of Dance in Los Angeles, she was determined to attend.

Miss Ruth

Ruth St. Denis was born in New Jersey and started out as a dancer in vaudeville shows that traveled throughout the country in circuits, or tours. Vaudeville shows featured many styles of entertaining dance, such as tap dancing, soft shoe, and acrobatic dance. But Miss Ruth wanted to dance in a more spiritual way. For inspiration, she looked to other cultures and countries, such as Egypt, India and those in the Far East, where dance had long been a respected part of religious observance. She began creating original dances inspired by aspects of the culture and dance from these far-away places.

Up until this time, the only dance that was well known in the United States

Pictured here are Ruth St. Denis and her husband, Ted Shawn, posing in Asian-inspired costumes around 1920. These two dance artists founded the Denishawn School of Dance in 1915. The school was known for offering a large variety of classes in dance from different countries. Martha Graham received her early dance training at the Denishawn School of Dance and performed with the Denishawn Dance Company.

was classical ballet and the styles featured in vaudeville. In contrast, Ruth St. Denis's barefoot dances created feelings of exotic mystery and calm. In the

American dancer and choreographer Isadora Duncan (pictured here on January 1, 1900) was an extremely important figure in the world of modern dance. Duncan's dances, which were very lyrical and expressive, were inspired by ancient Greek concepts of beauty.

Joining the Denishawn Family

In the summer of 1916, Graham arrived in Los Angeles to audition for the Denishawn school. In her book *Blood Memory*, she remembers being ushered into a room filled with green curtains where a man sat at a piano smoking a cigar. That man was Louis Horst, and he would later collaborate with Graham as well as become a close, personal friend. Miss Ruth appeared in the

early years of the twentieth century, her unusual performances were greeted with enthusiasm. Another famous dancer of this time period was Isadora Duncan, who, like Ruth St. Denis, danced barefoot and expressively. American dance was changing, and Martha Graham wanted to be a part of it.

room and asked Graham to dance for her. Martha did not know what to do. She had never had any dancing lessons. Miss Ruth asked Horst to play a waltz. Once the music began, Martha danced furiously, but when she was done, Miss Ruth did not seem very impressed. Miss Ruth decided not to teach Martha herself, but she allowed her to study at the school. Martha was disappointed not to be working with her idol, but she was happy enough to become a part of her world.

Denishawn was the first school in the United States to offer a diverse curriculum in dance training. The school was housed in a big mansion on top of a hill surrounded by eucalyptus trees. All of the students and faculty lived in the mansion. Miss Ruth owned exotic animals, such as peacocks, that wandered freely on the grounds. The dance classes were held outside on wooden platforms built over the tennis courts. Students attending Denishawn took a variety of different classes, such as classical ballet (although with bare feet); character dance; and dances from other countries such as China, Japan, and India. They learned philosophy, music, visual art, costume design and construction, dramatic gesture, lighting, and stage makeup. Even yoga and meditation were offered. Denishawn also had a successful dance company that toured the country performing Miss Ruth's and Ted Shawn's dances.

Unlikely Student

When Graham began her training, neither Miss Ruth nor Ted Shawn thought that she would ever perform. They did not think she was attractive or talented enough for an onstage career. They assumed she would become a teacher at Denishawn. Martha danced secretly at night. She would sneak downstairs and practice until dawn in Miss Ruth's private studio, trying to find her own unique way of dancing.

Graham continued to idolize Miss Ruth and appreciate her spiritual approach to dance performance and education. Miss Ruth realized, long before dance was an acceptable art form in the West, that dance spoke volumes about people, their culture, and their lives. Graham became Miss Ruth's special helper, sewing costumes for her solo concerts and going to church services with her on Sundays. She watched and learned to imitate everything Miss Ruth did: how she walked, danced, and spoke. But it was Ted Shawn who finally gave Martha the chance to dance.

Stepping In

Ted Shawn had choreographed a solo dance called *Seranata Morisca* (1917). One of the lead dancers in the company became sick and could not perform it. As Shawn tried to figure out who would replace her, he remarked that it was unfortunate Graham couldn't dance the piece. Graham insisted she could and proved it by immediately performing the dance. She had learned the choreography to the difficult solo by watching the other dancers practice. Graham danced the solo in San Diego at a gala performance. Shawn was impressed with her performance. He realized that the way Graham danced his choreography was how he had always wanted it to be performed. He began using her in many other dances.

In June 1920, inspired by Graham's dancing, Shawn created *Xochitl*, a dramatic piece about a Toltec Indian princess, with Martha dancing the title role. *Xochitl* was filled with dramatic dancing that told the story of the young Toltec princess who must fight off the advances of an Aztec emperor. After its premiere, Graham received rave reviews for her portrayal of the fiery character. As a result, *Xochitl* became an immediate success.

An old postcard from 1920 advertises Ted Shawn's famous dance, *Xochitl*. Because of her dynamic performance in this piece, Graham was noticed by theater producers in New York City. This was a very important step in her career.

Getting Noticed and Learning More

For the next three years, Graham danced and toured with the Denishawn Dance Company, performing *Xochitl* and other dances all across America and Europe. She received excellent reviews wherever they performed. Even with this success, Graham continued to be Miss Ruth's devoted helper, but this relationship was becoming somewhat difficult for her. Sometimes Graham even hid her reviews from Miss Ruth for fear that she would become jealous and send her away from Denishawn.

On the other hand, even though she did not respect him in the same way that she did Miss Ruth, Graham seemed to

Blazing Artistry

In her book *Blood Memory,* Martha says that critics wrote that she "blazed" when dancing *Xochitl* . This was always Graham's favorite review of her dancing. She described her interpretation of the role like this: "I was almost like an animal in my movements. I wanted to be a wild, beautiful creature, maybe of another world—but very, very wild."

understand how to help Ted Shawn make his dances better. Soon she was given more responsibility within the company. If Miss Ruth and Ted were not going to travel with the company on a tour, Graham would be put in charge of the company. During these times, Graham had the added administrative responsibilities of managing the company while she was performing. She also began to teach at the Denishawn school. Graham would draw from all of these experiences later, when she formed her own company.

After three years of all these responsibilities Graham was beginning to outgrow Denishawn. One critic wrote after a performance in New York City in the early 1920s that Graham was the only dancer in the company to dance with passion and excitement. As Graham says in her book *Blood Memory*, "This of course, did not sit too well with either Miss Ruth or Ted." In 1923, when the Denishawn Dance Company was preparing to tour Asia, Graham was not invited to go with them.

At the time, there was a vaudeville revue in New York called the Greenwich Village Follies. The producer for this show, John Murray Anderson, had seen Graham dance with Denishawn. Impressed, he invited her to join the Greenwich Village Follies in 1923. Like her idol Miss Ruth, Graham did not think of herself as an entertainer. She thought of herself as an artist. She

didn't want to be a part of vaudeville. But she needed an income, and the Follies were going to pay her $350 a week, which was considered a large sum of money in those days. Martha accepted Mr. Anderson's offer.

The Greenwich Village Follies

Graham became the lead dancer in the Follies. She choreographed many of her own dances, but they were similar to those she had done with Denishawn. She also had to perform many of the solos she had done with Denishawn, including *Seranata Morisca*. Although she wanted to branch out and be more creative, Mr. Anderson insisted that Graham stick with the Denishawn style.

Graham tended to separate herself from the vaudeville dancers in the Follies. She refused to be a part of the finale where the girls paraded across the stage in fancy and often scanty costumes. The show's producers threatened to remove Graham's solo dances from the program unless she participated in the finale, but Graham still refused. The producers cut her solos, but after a few nights, brought them back because of the audience demand.

Graham grew increasingly more frustrated with the Follies and the restraints they imposed on her creativity. After two seasons, she quit in search of new experiences and artistic freedom. She was ready to create her own dances.

3 New Frontiers

In 1925, when Graham left the Follies, she accepted a teaching job at the Eastman School of Music in Rochester, New York, where a new dance program had been established. She had her own students, her own studio, and finally, the artistic freedom to create all of her own dances. She made the overnight commute from New York City twice a week along with pianist and composer Louis Horst, who had also left Denishawn.

At Eastman, Martha continued to search for her own particular style of dancing—something unique, American, and totally honest in its expression of human emotions. She made some progress here, but she found the audience in Rochester uninterested in her dance experiments. When asked to return for a second year of teaching at Eastman, she declined. Martha knew she needed to be in the center of the art world, and New York City was where she would find it.

The Eastman School of Music, where Martha Graham taught, was home to the Eastman Theater (pictured here in August 1922). The theater was the first performance space owned and run by a university in the United States. The theater, which was able to seat an audience of up to 3,400 people, was filled with wonderful marble, rare woods, paintings, sculptures, and bronze statues.

In New York, Martha had very little money, but she knew that she had to present her work to the public if she wanted to succeed. She borrowed money to help fund her first public performance.

Martha then went to one of her former employers from the Greenwich Village Follies and asked him if she could use his theater to present one night of her dancing. His response was that she could do so under one condition. If her performance was not a success, she would have to sign another yearlong contract to perform in the Greenwich Village Follies. She agreed. Graham's one chance to present herself to the public would be exceedingly important.

Success!

This performance on April 18, 1926 (when Graham was thirty-two years old), included Graham and three women who had been her students at Eastman. She billed them as Martha Graham and Dance Group. Graham choreographed eighteen short dances and, together with her dancers, created and sewed all of the costumes for the performance. Louis Horst accompanied the four women on the piano. Some of the pieces Graham presented that evening included *Chorale*, *Clair de Lune*, *Desir*, and *Tanagra*. Although there was a late spring snowstorm that evening, the theater was filled with curious people who responded passionately to what they witnessed. Some people loved the performance. Others hated it. But no one could dismiss it.

As soon as the concert was over, Graham began planning her next one. It didn't matter to her if the audience loved or hated her work, just as long as they felt something. As long as there was an audience, she would dance for them. In order to develop her work and create new dances, Graham knew she needed to continue exploring movement in her own body and to share this exploration with other dancers. In 1926, she opened her own school, the Martha Graham School for Contemporary Dance.

Rebel

Alone and with her students, Graham explored how movement could express all the emotions of the human heart. At that time, classical ballet technique was the most popular technique used to develop dancers for the stage. To this day, when anyone watches a ballet performance, the dancers they see convey a sense of weightlessness. Graham did not always want her dancers to appear weightless. Nor did she want her dancing to always appear "easy." Graham believed that life and its experiences required effort and she was determined to change the opinion that showing this effort was a bad thing.

Graham thought a lot about what happened in her body when she was breathing. She noticed that there are many different ways to breathe. For example, sighing, gasping, shuddering, sobbing, and laughing are all ways of expressing emotion and involve different patterns of

In this photo from 1927, Graham demonstrates a version of the movement she called a contraction. Contraction, along with its opposite movement, release, constitute the basic movements of the modern dance technique Graham pioneered.

breathing. Martha believed that by connecting breath and movement, her dancing could become more meaningful and expressive. The new dance technique Martha developed was founded on the two basic movements that occur in every breath: contraction and release. During exhalation, the deep muscles of the torso contract, forcing the air out of the lungs. During inhalation, the same muscles release as fresh air rushes back in. Graham taught her dancers to curve their spines forward, sideward, or backward around the exhalation creating a dynamic impulse for movement that continued to flow through the body as the muscles released during inhalation.

Between 1926 and 1930, she created almost eighty new dances using her new expressive technique and language of movement.

Many of them were unlike anything audiences had ever seen before. Her dancers pushed against the air with flexed feet and moved their torsos in percussive bursts of angular shapes. They fell to the floor, quivered, and trembled as they expressed the full range of human feeling in Graham's dances. These dances were about issues that had not previously been addressed through dance. Some of her dances made social or political statements. For example, *Poems of 1917* was an antiwar dance. *Adolescence* addressed the problems that young girls face during their preteen years. *Heretic*, a striking image of intolerance, pitted a solo figure in white against a group of black-robed opponents.

Teaching, Sharing, and Learning

Like her choreography, Graham's classes were exciting and dynamic. More and more dancers began to come to her studio. Over the years, many famous dancers who would later become choreographers studied with her, including Alvin Ailey, Twyla Tharp, Paul Taylor, and Merce Cunningham. At the Neighborhood Playhouse, an acting school in New York City where Graham taught actors how to use their bodies as expressive instruments, she also had many famous pupils, including Bette

Twyla Tharp (*left*) is shown here rehearsing her dance *Eight Jelly Rolls*. When she was a young dancer in New York City, Tharp studied modern dance with Martha Graham. Today, Tharp's choreography is characterized by its mixture of ballet, jazz, and modern dance.

Davis, Kirk Douglas, and Woody Allen.

Graham began all of her classes seated on the floor. There, her students performed warm-up exercises, called floor work, designed to stretch and strengthen the spine and legs. After the floor work, the students would rise to their feet and work on balancing and strengthening exercises. Graham wanted them to feel a connection with the floor and with the earth. Graham respected the natural force of gravity and taught her students new movements that pulled them low to the floor. The classes ended with the students walking, leaping, skipping, and jumping across the floor.

Graham chose the dancers for her company from among her students. She worked her dancers hard. Often, when she was creating a new dance, they would stay in the studio through the night. They were disciplined and devoted to Graham's technique. They were proud and honored to be helping her create her new, fiercely dramatic, and emotional repertoire of dances.

During the same time that Graham was creating her new dance technique, she was also experimenting with music and costuming for her dances. Louis Horst, who continued to accompany her classes, became the musical director for her company. He taught Graham about musical form and encouraged her to work with contemporary composers rather than making dances to eighteenth- and nineteenth-century music as St. Denis and Duncan had done. Graham collaborated with many of the most famous American composers of her time, including Aaron Copland and Samuel Barber. Graham also designed and created costumes and makeup for her dances. In doing so, she was able to ensure that every theatrical element supported her choreographic ideas.

Early Masterpieces

From 1927 through 1935, Martha choreographed many dances that audiences would respond to passionately for decades. In 1930, she created a solo called *Lamentation*. In it, the dancer sits on a bench throughout the entire dance, encased in a long tube-like costume that represents the sadness that engulfs a person who is lamenting a loss or death. The dancer twists her torso as she tilts to one direction and then another, stretching the fabric as if trying to break free from grief. The striking costuming and seated dance were both original for their time.

In the early 1930s, Graham visited New Mexico, where she saw American Indian rituals. Soon after, she began choreographing a dance that was inspired by Southwestern American Indian religious rites that celebrated the Virgin Mary. Graham worked on the dance for a long time. This dance, called *Primitive Mysteries*, is a study in choreographic simplicity and elegance. Throughout its three sections, a group of young women in long, dark blue dresses worship the Virgin, a central figure dressed in a white organza gown. She, in

In 1986, American artist Andy Warhol who is especially well-known for his silkscreen images of celebrities such as Marilyn Monroe and objects such as a Campbell's soup can paid tribute to Martha Graham and her dance *Lamentation*. This serigraph is one of three of the *Martha Graham Portfolio* that Warhol created.

turn, embraces them in tender compassion, bestowing blessings and invoking their praise with her silent weight shifts and stylized hand gestures. The thumping sound of the dancers' footsteps as their movement evolves from a simple walking procession to more complex circular patterns of jumps, falls, and tilted angular shapes becomes part of the sparse score for flute, oboe, and percussion composed by Louis Horst. At its premiere in 1931, *Primitive Mysteries* received more than thirty curtain calls. Audiences and critics declared this new work a masterpiece. Years later, Graham described the dance as a celebration of the young girls she portrayed in the dance. Graham's depiction of the Virgin paralleled reality as she herself became celebrated throughout the world as a dancer and choreographer.

The solo dance *Frontier*, choreographed in 1935, is a celebration of the American pioneer woman. The little jumps, repeated running patterns, and sweeping circular kicks evoke the courageous, optimistic character of all American women who helped settle the country. Isamu Noguchi, a Japanese American sculptor, designed the simple three-dimensional sculptural set that represented the expanse of the American plains. His design revolutionized set design on the American stage. Graham would continue to collaborate with Noguchi for more than fifty years.

4 A Legend's Work

Throughout the 1930s, Graham choreographed almost fifty new dances. Students were flocking to her studio to study with her. One day, a handsome, classically trained ballet dancer named Erick Hawkins began taking her classes. Martha was deeply attracted to his strong, masculine dancing and dashing good looks. He eventually became the first male member of her company, dancing leading roles opposite Graham. With Hawkins, Graham began to explore new relationships in her dances. She was now beginning to explore the struggles and pleasures of romantic love through her choreography.

New Dynamics Need New Forms

She was also experimenting with new theatrical elements. In *American Document* (1938) and *Letter to the World* (1940), Graham combined spoken word with dance.

Martha Graham is pictured rehearsing in New York City in May 1950, with her dance partner Erick Hawkins. The first male dancer in Graham's dance company, Hawkins was born in 1909, in Colorado, and died in 1994.

American Document was a celebration of American freedom and values that incorporated readings from the Declaration of Independence, Walt Whitman's *Leaves of Grass*, and the Bible together with music and dance. Audiences related to *American Document* and, in turn, became more accepting of modern dance. *Letter to the World*, a dance-biography of the American poet Emily Dickinson, fused Dickinson's poetry with music and dance. Graham was starting a new trend of dance-theater that audiences loved.

Love and Heartbreak

In the 1940s, fueled by her love for Hawkins, Graham created many of her most popular works. *Appalachian Spring* (1944), with music commissioned by Aaron Copland, explores

Martha Graham with Erick Hawkins and other dancers photographed in *Appalachian Spring*. The photo dates from January 1, 1945. Graham's collaboration with composer Aaron Copland and sculptor Isamu Noguchi, who created the expressionistic set design for the piece, led to the creation of this American modern dance masterpiece.

the American dream. It follows a young pioneer couple celebrating the beginning of their new life. Graham danced the role of the young bride, and Erick Hawkins danced the role of her husband. In *Cave of the Heart* (1946), Graham told the Greek story of Medea, a woman who discovers that her husband, Jason, has been unfaithful to her. Medea takes revenge by killing her children and presenting them to Jason. Once again, Graham and Hawkins played opposite each other. Their passionate personal relationship brought great drama to the roles they danced on stage.

Diversion of Angels (1948), a joyous, lyrical dance about love, became another audience favorite. The same summer that *Diversion of Angels* premiered, Graham and Hawkins secretly eloped in

The American Dancer

Graham's popularity continued to grow throughout the 1930s and 1940s. In 1937, she was the first American dancer to be invited to the White House. First Lady Eleanor Roosevelt extended the invitation, and Graham made quite an impression performing three solos for the president. She and Mrs. Roosevelt became good friends, and Graham would dance for seven more presidents at the White House.

Santa Fe, New Mexico. Graham was fifty-four years old. Though Graham and Hawkins tried to make their marriage work, it was a competitive relationship filled with conflict. During the spring of 1950, the company began its first European tour. Graham severely injured her knee. This had devastating results. If Graham was not on stage, the audiences were not interested. Shortly after her injury, the tour ended. Hawkins left the company and their marriage. Graham was now fifty-six. She began to face the daunting reality that she would not be able to dance forever. Heartbroken and injured, Graham returned home alone.

Moving On

After her knee healed, Martha threw herself into her work. She returned to her theme of the spiritual and emotional struggles and triumphs of women. In 1955, she created another of her best-known works, *Seraphic Dialogue*, based on the life of Joan of Arc. In that same year, Graham was asked by the government of the United States to tour Asia and the Middle East as a representative of the American spirit and the American people. She traveled with her company for four months, speaking and giving interviews during the day and dancing every night. Even at sixty-two years old, her strength and energy surpassed that of the younger dancers in her company. Having the opportunity to visit Eastern countries such as Japan, Indonesia, India, Pakistan, and Iran, and introduce them to her dancing thrilled Graham because she always had a deep respect for Asian philosophy. During her lifetime, she and her company would tour Europe, the Middle East, and Asia many more times.

The 1960s were a challenging time for Graham. Her dear friend Louis Horst passed away, as did her mother. And she was starting to realize that she was too old to continue to dance. Graham wrestled with this reality throughout the decade, as she fought an addiction to alcohol that contributed to her depression and ill health. For a time, Graham would not leave her home to attend rehearsals or her company's performances. Eventually, she pulled herself out of her depression and gave her final performance in 1969. In *A Time of Snow*, at the age of seventy-five, she portrayed an elderly woman, Heloise, looking back on her life.

A Lasting Legacy

After retiring from the stage, Graham continued to choreograph. At first, it was frustrating and difficult for her to create dances in which she had no performing role. Graham had always thought of herself as a dancer first and a choreographer second. But from 1973 until her death, Graham created more than twenty new dances and revived many of her older works for her company. Her version of Stravinsky's *Rite of Spring*, which she choreographed in 1984, is considered by many critics to be among her greatest works. She continued to speak at her company's performances as well as give lectures about her art. A striking woman, she never stopped fascinating and enticing her audiences.

In the late 1970s and 1980s, Graham worked with many famous performers outside the world of modern dance. Ballet stars Rudolf Nureyev and Mikhail Baryshnikov danced in revivals of her work. The Broadway, film, and TV star Liza Minelli worked closely with her, and the girl who would become the pop

Advice to Young Artists

Shortly after her death, *Blood Memory*, (1991), a memoir of Graham's life and work was published. In it, she gives this advice to young artists: "There is only one of you in the world, just one, and if that is not fulfilled then something has been lost."

In 2004, the U.S. Postal Service released a series of stamps featuring great American choreographers of the twentieth century. In addition to the stamp honoring Martha Graham, the series includes images of Agnes de Mille, George Balanchine, and Alvin Ailey.

star Madonna was her student.

In October 1990, Graham's last complete work, *Maple Leaf Rag*, premiered in New York. Based on a joyful tune that Louis Horst played for Graham more than fifty years earlier whenever she needed cheering up, the choreography was a joyous reflection of Graham's own life and experiences. Martha Graham died on April 1, 1991, at the age of ninety-six. Newspaper headlines cried out the news of her death to the world, declaring her life and work as "revolutionary" to the dance world.

In fact, Graham's influence reached far beyond the dance community and managed to penetrate the entire world. Her dances are still performed worldwide, and her company still tours the world. Martha Graham's example of dedication, commitment, and passion speaks volumes about the capabilities of the human spirit. She forged her path on the earth by her dedication to the art of dance, and she changed that art forever.

Glossary

character dance A dance that utilizes the music and folk movements of a particular country, or reveals the occupation or age of the performer's character.

choreographer Someone who creates dances.

choreography The art of arranging movement into dances.

contraction In the Graham Technique™, the letting out of breath in a specific way in order to initiate movement.

elope To secretly marry, or travel away together to be wed.

gala performance A celebratory performance that usually starts a companys' season in a specific city. Many benefactors, supporters, and famous people attend.

mentor A teacher, or guide in life.

pioneer A person who ventures into unknown territory.

soft shoe A style of dance related to tap dancing but performed in soft-soled shoes.

vaudeville A stage show that offers a variety of short acts.

For More Information

Web Sites

Due to the changing nature of Internet links, the Rosen Publishing Group, Inc., has developed an online list of Web sites related to the subject of this book. This site is updated regularly. Please use this link to access the list:

http://www.rosenlinks.com/lac/magr

For Further Reading

The Curtain Call Library of Dance Series. New York, NY: The Rosen Publishing Group, Inc.

Freedman, Russell. *Martha Graham: A Dancer's Life*. New York, NY: Houghton Mifflin Company, 1998.

Garfunkel, Trudy. *Letter to the World: The Life and Dances of Martha Graham*. Boston, MA: Little, Brown & Company, 1995.

Graham, Martha. *Blood Memory*. New York, NY: Bantam Doubleday Dell Publishing Group, Inc., 1991.

Bibliography

De Mille, Agnes. *The Life and Work of Martha Graham*. New York, NY: Random House, Inc., 1956.

Freedman, Russel. *Martha Graham: A Dancer's Life*. New York, NY: Houghton Mifflin Company, 1998.

Garfunkel, Trudy. *The Life and Dances of Martha Graham*. Boston, MA: Little, Brown & Company, 1995.

Graham, Martha. *Blood Memory*. New York, NY: Bantam Doubleday Dell Publishing Group, Inc., 1991.

Solomon Probosz, Kathilyn. *Martha Graham* New York, NY: Simon & Schuster, 1995.

Index

About the Author

Kristin Kessel Martine has a master of arts in dance and dance education from New York University and an undergraduate degree in theater and speech from Wagner College. She has written for *Pointe* magazine and has also authored *Dance Performance: From Rehearsal to Opening Night* as part of the Curtain Call Library of Dance series. She currently teaches dance in a high school performing arts program in New York.

Photo Credits

Cover, p. 5 © Everett Collection; cover (background), p. 1 © Jerry Cooke/Corbis; pp. 6, 9, 22 © Jerome Robbins Dance Division, The New York Public Library for the Performing Arts, Astor, Lenox and Tilden Foundations; pp. 13, 27, 30 © Bettmann/Corbis; pp. 14, 38 © AP/Wide World Photos; p. 17 © Ed Hoppé/Corbis; p. 18 © Hulton Archive/Getty Images; p. 32 © Gjon Mili/Time Life Pictures/Getty Images; p. 35 © Andy Warhol Foundation/Corbis; p. 39 © Jerry Cooke/Pix Inc./Time Life Pictures; p. 44 © United States Postal Service.

Designer: Tahara Anderson;
Developmental Editor: Nancy Allison, CMA, RME